Little Mitchie

LET'S LOOK INSIDE A SCHOOL BUS

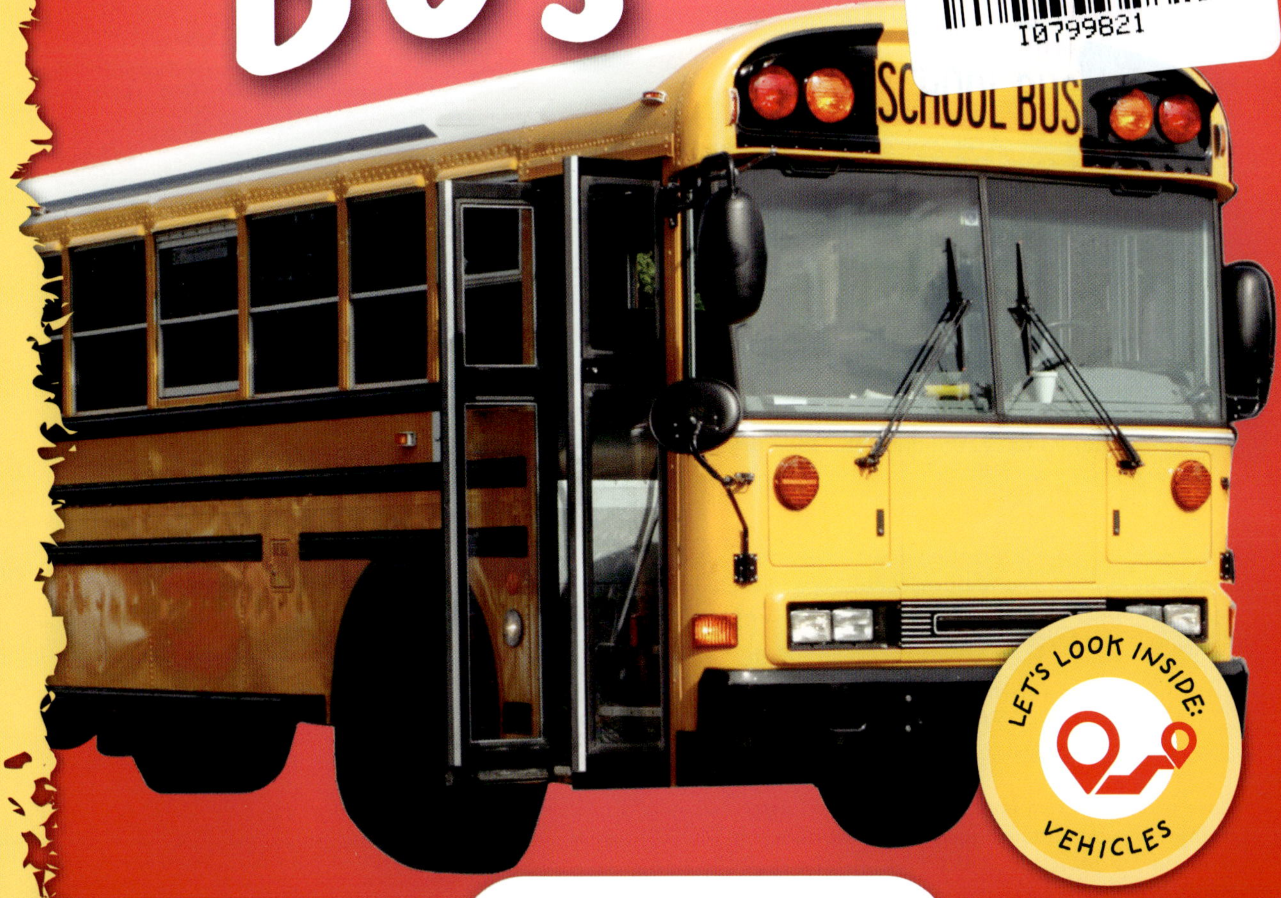

LET'S LOOK INSIDE: VEHICLES

PAUL ZACHARY

CREATING YOUNG NONFICTION READERS

Little Mitchie books spark curiosity and support early nonfiction reading for students in Grades 2-3. Designed to build vocabulary, support second language learners, and prepare readers for middle-grade content, each book includes helpful tips for parents and educators to build confidence and deepen understanding of the world.

TIPS FOR READING NONFICTION WITH BEGINNING READERS

Talk about Nonfiction

Begin by explaining that nonfiction books give us information that is true. The book will be organized around a specific topic or idea, and we may learn new facts through reading.

Look at the Parts

Most nonfiction books have helpful features. Our *Little Mitchie* titles include color photographs and graphic aids, a table of contents, a glossary, and an index. Share the purpose of these features with your reader.

Color Photos and Graphic Aids

A lot of information can be found by "reading" photos, charts, maps, and other graphic aids found within nonfiction texts. Help your reader learn more about the different ways information can be displayed.

Table of Contents

Located at the front of the book, this list shows the big ideas within the text and the page numbers where they can be found.

Glossary

Located at the back of the book, the glossary defines key words and phrases that are related to the topic. These words and phrases can be found in the text in colored type.

Index

Located at the back of the book, an index is an alphabetical list of topics and the page numbers where they can be found.

With a little help and guidance about reading nonfiction, you can feel good about introducing a young reader to the world of *Little Mitchie* nonfiction books.

Little Mitchie is an imprint of:

Mitchell Lane
PUBLISHERS

2001 SW 31st Avenue
Hallandale, FL 33009
mitchelllanepub.com

First Edition, 2027.

Author: Paul Zachary
Designer: Rhea Magaro
Editor: Tricia Hoffman

Library of Congress Cataloging-in-Publication Data
Title: Let's Look Inside a School Bus / by Paul Zachary.

Description: Hallandale, FL :
Mitchell Lane Publishers, [2027]

Identifiers:
ISBN 979-8-89260-879-4 (library bound)
ISBN 979-8-90145-049-9 (paperback)
ISBN 979-8-89260-982-1 (eBook)

Library of Congress Control Number: 2026930268

Photo credits: Alamy: Marcio Silva, 5; Shutterstock: Le Do, 1, 3, 4, 9, 14; Stuart Monk, 6; Drazen Zigic, 8; LightField Studios, 10, 11; Prostock-studio, 12; Luna Yimo, 15; ND700, 16; PBL Boards and Gifts, 19; 4 PM production, 21; Rob Wilson, 22

TABLE OF CONTENTS

Chapter One

ALL ABOARD

Here comes the big yellow school bus, rolling down the street. It carries students to and from school every day. The bus helps students get to school—and back home—safely.

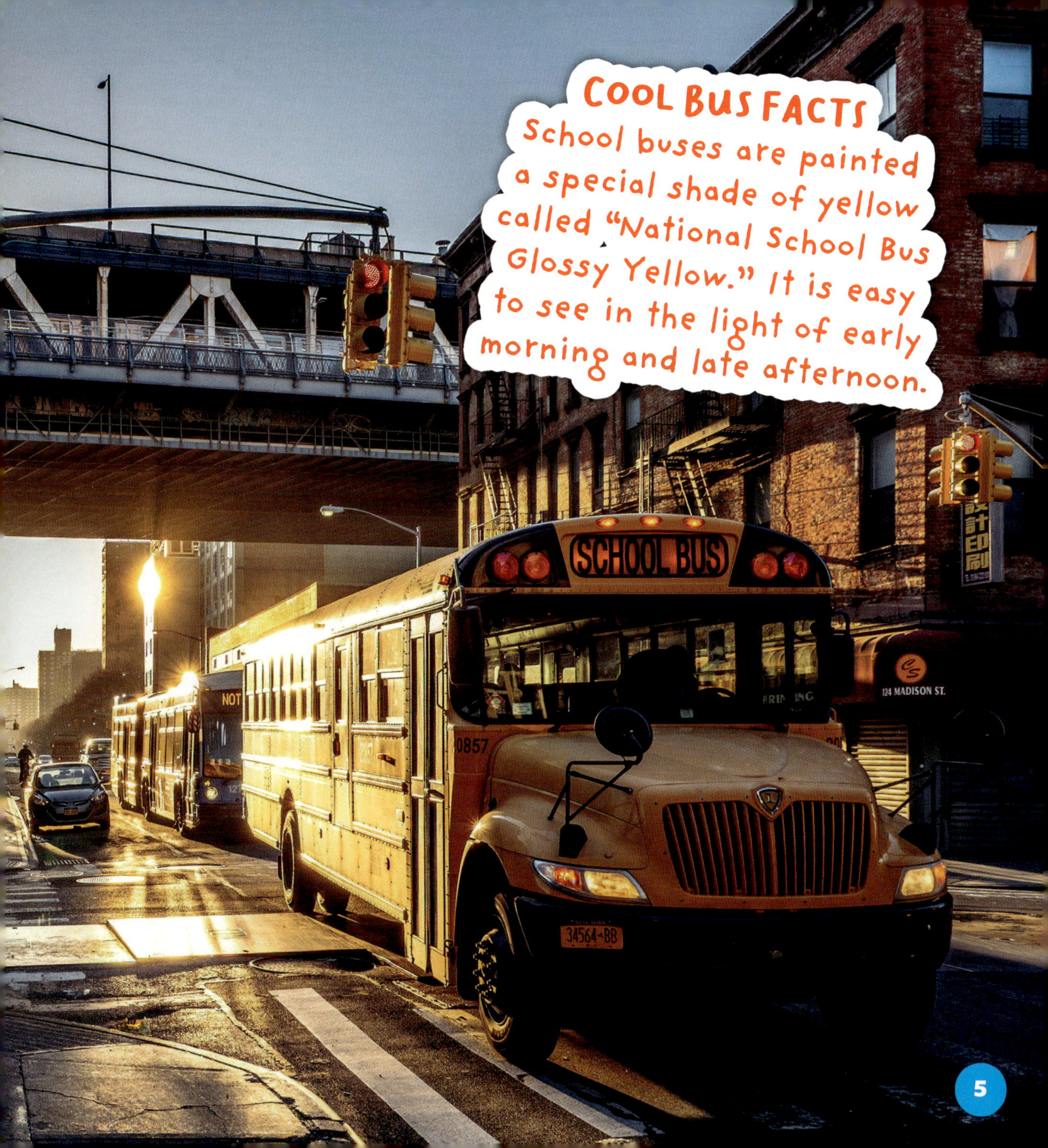

COOL BUS FACTS

School buses are painted a special shade of yellow called "National School Bus Glossy Yellow." It is easy to see in the light of early morning and late afternoon.

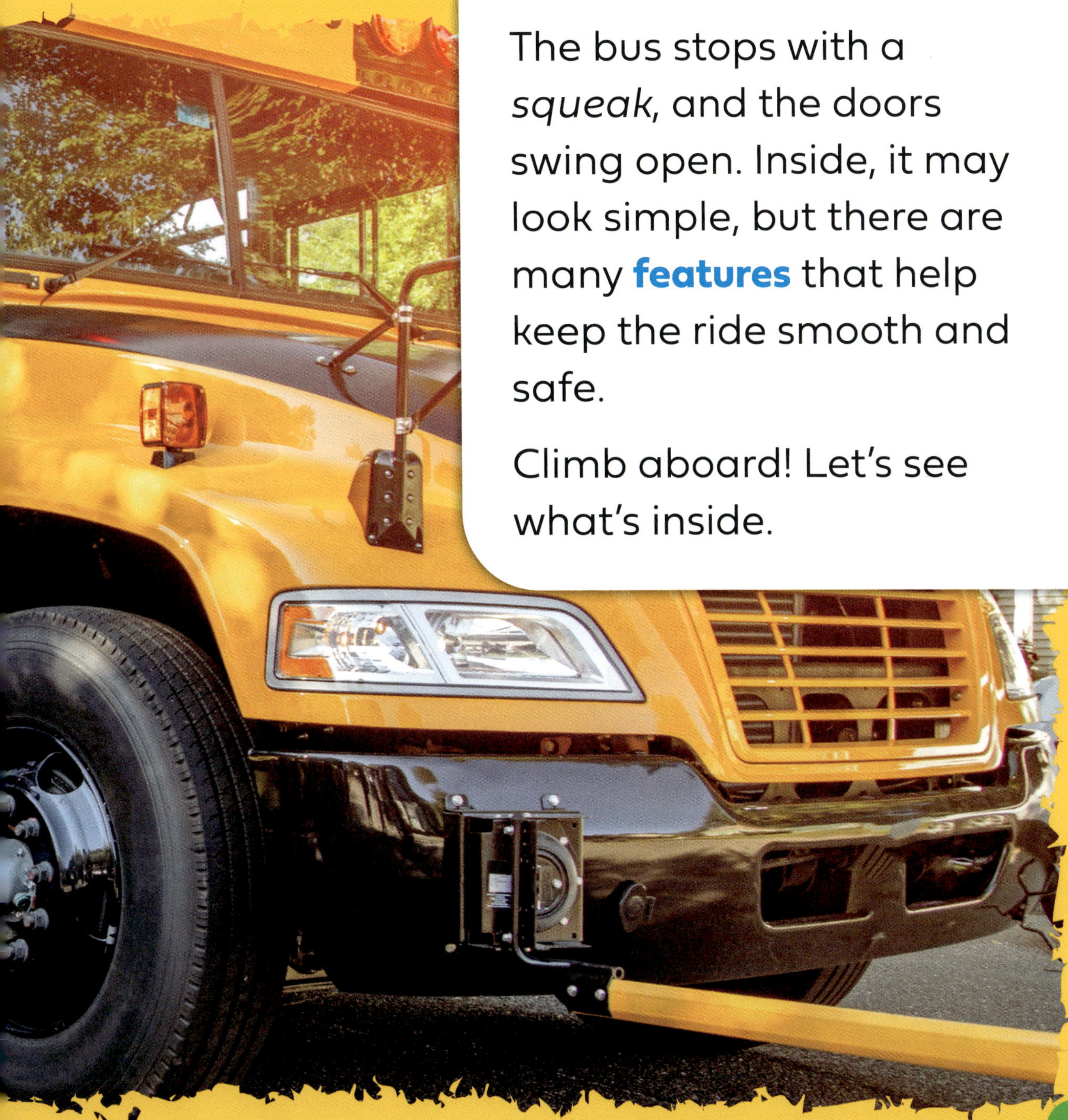

The bus stops with a *squeak*, and the doors swing open. Inside, it may look simple, but there are many **features** that help keep the ride smooth and safe.

Climb aboard! Let's see what's inside.

Chapter Two

THE DRIVER'S CONTROLS

At the front of the bus is the driver's seat. The bus driver uses many important **controls**. There is a steering wheel. There is a gas pedal. There are buttons for the lights and the horn. *Honk!*

The driver uses a large **lever** to open and close the bus door. This helps students get on and off the bus easily.

The driver has an important job. She makes sure the bus stays on the road, stops safely, and watches out for students getting on and off the bus.

COOL BUS FACTS

Bus drivers must complete special training and pass tests before they can drive a school bus. They learn how to keep students safe on every trip.

Chapter Three

SEATS AND SAFETY

Inside the school bus, rows of seats line both sides of the **aisle**. Two or three students sit in each seat, chatting and laughing together. Each seat is **designed** to keep students safe if the bus stops suddenly. Some buses have **seat belts** too!

COOL BUS FACTS

Handrails and steps help children get on and off carefully. The bus also has emergency exits, including windows and doors that can open if needed.

STOP

The bus hums and bumps along the road. When it stops to pick up or drop off students, its red lights flash. A large red stop sign swings out from the side of the bus. All other cars on the road must stop and wait.

There is an emergency exit in the back of the bus. It's a special door that students can use—just in case!

EMERGENCY DOOR
260723

Chapter Four

A SAFE RIDE

The yellow bus is more than just a vehicle—it's a place where friends meet and laugh. Every trip brings a little fun and adventure on the way to school.

COOL BUS FACTS

School buses are one of the safest ways for children to travel to school.

A LOOK INSIDE

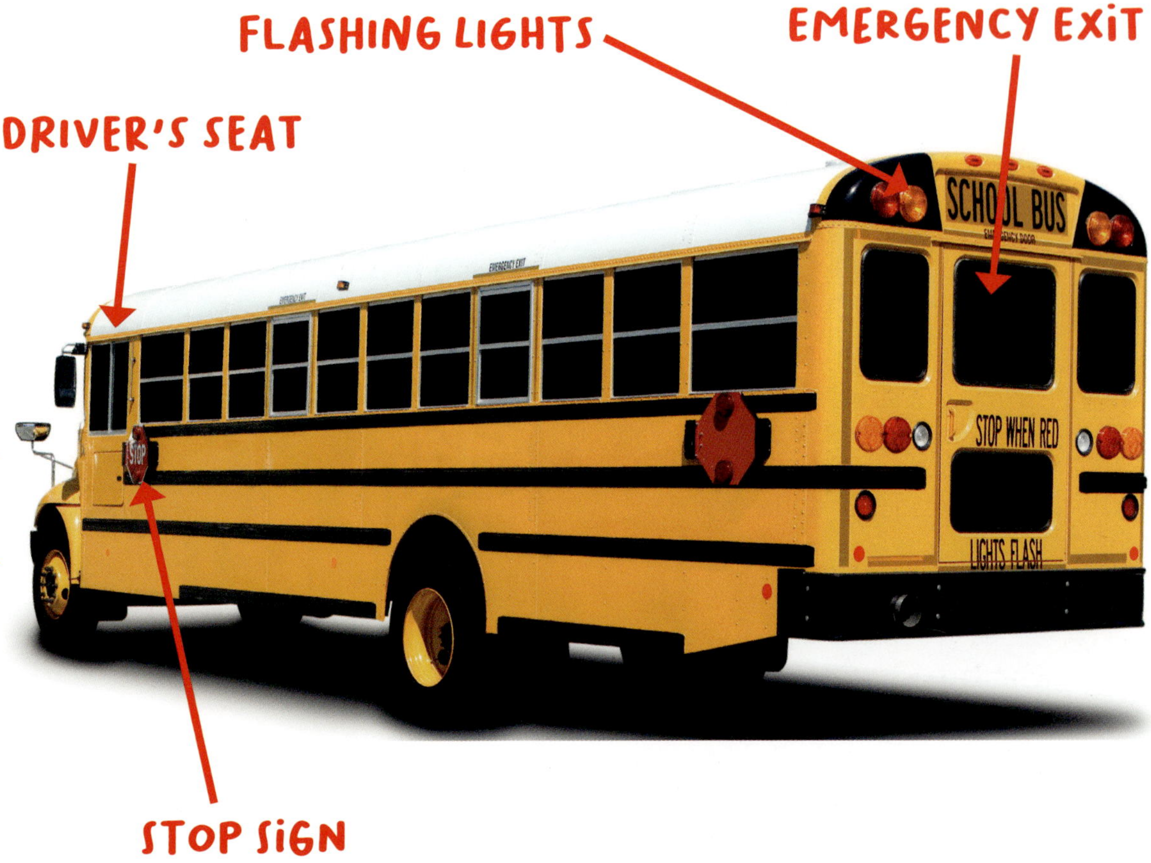

GLOSSARY

aisle (ile) the space between rows of seats where people walk

controls (kuhn-trohlz) the buttons, pedals, and steering wheel the driver uses to move and stop the bus

designed (di-zined) made or planned for a special purpose

emergency (i-mur-juhn-see) a sudden problem or danger that needs help right away

features (fee-churz) important parts or special things about something

handrail (hand-rayl) a bar that people can hold onto for support

lever (lev-ur) a handle the driver moves to open or close the bus doors

seat belt (seet belt) a strap that keeps passengers safe in their seats

FURTHER READING

Deniston, Natalie. *School Buses.* Jump!, Inc., 2025.

Sanderson, Whitney. *First Ride on a School Bus with Tamir.* Lerner Publications, 2026.

ON THE INTERNET

School Bus Depot

www.pbs.org/video/kidvision-vpk-school-bus-depot/

Watch a short video as kids learn about school bus safety.

School Bus Safety

https://csn.org/bus/

This page includes explanations of how buses are built to be safe and why laws protect children getting on and off the bus.

INDEX